P9-AQW-248

A Civilization Project Book

ANCIENT GREECE

BY SUSAN PURDY
AND CASS R. SANDAK

Illustrations and diagrams by Bert Dodson

WITHDRAWN

Franklin Watts New York/London/Toronto/Sydney 1982

PROPERTY OF
FAUQUIER COUNTY PUBLIC LIBRARY

Contents

Library of Congress Cataloging in Publication Data

Purdy, Susan Gold
  Ancient Greece.
  (A Civilization project book)
  Includes index.
  Summary: Briefly describes ancient Greek civilization and provides instructions for making models of items such as Greek columns, statues, stringed instruments, and catapults.
    1. Civilization, Greek—Juvenile literature.
2. Handicraft—Juvenile literature. [1. Civilization, Greek. 2. Handicraft. 3. Models and modelmaking]
I. Sandak, Cass R. II. Title. III. Series.
DF79.P84   938'.00228   82-7109
ISBN 0-531-04453-X   AACR2

Text and illustrations copyright © 1982 by Franklin Watts
All rights reserved
Printed in the United States of America
6   5

J
938
PUR

The Land and People of Ancient Greece

Ancient Greece included not only the rocky peninsula of modern Greece in southern Europe and the many clusters of islands in the Ionian and Aegean seas but also provinces and settlements in Asia Minor (modern Turkey).

The mainland of Greece consisted of two principal sections connected by the very narrow Isthmus of Corinth. Most of the major cities were in the northern section. The southern section—called the Peloponnesus—was the site of the ancient city of Sparta.

The first great period of civilization to develop in this area was the Mycenean Age. The people of the city of Mycenae flourished between 1600 and 1200 B.C. They left behind impressive architectural remains, including fortified palaces and massive tombs. Around 1200 B.C., invasions by northern Greek tribes led to a decline in the civilization. This period—until around 800 B.C.—is called the Dark Age of ancient Greek history and little is known about it. For a time, the art of writing was lost. Few works of art have survived.

Around 800 B.C., the poet Homer lived. He put together the oral legends of the Trojan War and composed the two great epics called *The Iliad* and *The Odyssey*. Homer gives us an insight into ancient warfare and heroic life.

The Greeks became expert sailors, traders, warriors, and colonists. They spread their language and culture to many Mediterranean lands and as far as the coasts of Spain, France, and North Africa. All the Greeks who lived in colonies scattered throughout the ancient world were united by a special feeling of being Greek. They all spoke dialects of the Greek language and shared common beliefs and traditions.

Because they were cut off from each other by mountains, hills, and the sea, each Greek community developed into an independent city-state, or *polis*. These city-states were largely self-sufficient. At first the city-states were ruled by an aristocracy of wealthy and powerful families. When the common people became rebellious, they chose their own leaders—called *tyrants*—to rule them. After the tyrants showed that they wanted too much power, *democracy* developed. Now all citizens were able to take part in decisions that affected the life of the city-state.

Athens, Thebes, Sparta, and Corinth were the most important city-states, and Athens was by far the most advanced of all of these. Greek civilization, philosophy, science, literature, and art were largely the creations of Athenians.

Life in ancient Greece was pleasant. Houses were comfortable. The climate was mild and people spent time outdoors. Children had many toys and playthings. Generally, only boys went to school. Greek girls were usually taught at home by their mothers, who were in charge of raising children, running the households, and supervising servants.

Sports, games, and athletic contests were an important part of life in the Greek city-states. The first Olympic games were held in 776 B.C. in honor of Zeus, king of the Greek gods. They were held every four years until A.D. 394—a period of nearly 1,200 years!

The city-states continued to develop until armies from Persia threatened to conquer the Greek mainland. After the Persian Wars (499–449 B.C.), Greece—and particularly Athens—entered its most glorious period. This was, the Golden Age of Greek

civilization. In the Classical Period (about 480–300 B.C.), Greek artists and sculptors tried to show both the natural and ideal in a balanced way. Later, emotion became more important than idealized perfection.

The chief works of Greek architecture were built between 700 B.C. and 146 B.C. After this period, the Romans gained complete political control of Greece. But the Roman world continued to look up to Greek civilization. In A.D. 395, the Roman Empire was split into two parts. The eastern portion of the empire continued for another thousand years, and continued to keep the Greek language and culture alive.

Greece and Asia Minor

Terra-cotta Figure Art

Greek potters used a reddish terra-cotta clay. They decorated their pottery in two basic styles. In the "red-figure" method, the figures were outlined, allowing the reddish background of the clay to show through the surrounding black glaze. In the "black-figure" method, the Athenian specialty, the figures were painted in black silhouette and the reddish background was allowed to show. Pottery designs portrayed gods and goddesses as well as scenes from everyday life. From the sixth century B.C. on, Greek potters were famous for their vases and bowls, which they exported throughout the ancient world.

These drawing activities, similar to the Greek potters' art, can be done with real terra-cotta clay and black glaze, or with paper and paint.

Materials you will need:
Terra-cotta colored paper, pencil, black ink, oaktag or poster board, terra-cotta colored crayon, black india ink and brush, toothpick or scratching tool

A. For the "black-figure" method:

1. Sketch a design on terra-cotta colored paper.

2. Paint the figures and designs in black outline.

3. Fill in the figures with black, but allow thin lines of terra-cotta to show through to define the details. Leave the background a terra-cotta color. (See Figure 1.)

4. Paint a decorative border around the picture.

Figure 1

B. For the "red-figure" method:

1. Sketch your design on terra-cotta colored paper.

2. Paint the background black. Leave people, trees, and other figures the terra-cotta color. Use thin black lines to show details. (See Figure 2.)

C. For the scratchboard technique, use oaktag or poster board with a shiny surface.

1. Cover the paper with terra-cotta colored crayon, making a solid area of color.

2. Cover the crayon-colored area with a layer or two of black india ink. Apply the ink with the brush.

Figure 2

3. When the ink is completely dry, scratch your design through the black layer with a toothpick or a sharp tool, exposing the red layer below. (See Figure 3.) This method is similar to the one the Greeks used when they scratched through the black pottery glaze to expose the red clay underneath.

Figure 3

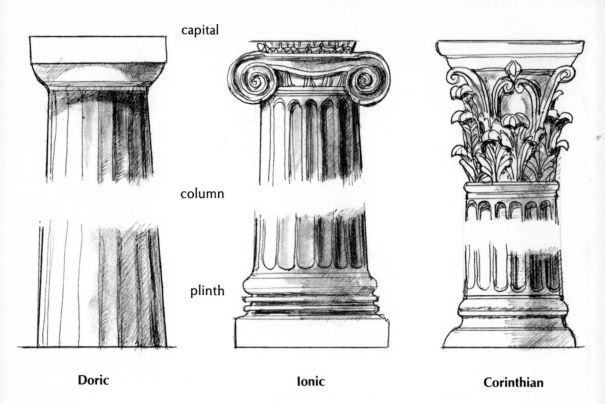

capital

column

plinth

Doric   **Ionic**   **Corinthian**

Making a
Classic Column

The most distinctive external features of the Greek temples were the columns. In early Greek history, there were only two main styles of architecture: Doric and Ionic. From the fifth century B.C. on, the Corinthian style was also popular. The names Doric, Ionic, and Corinthian denote the geographical area in which the architectural forms were most frequently found.

The Doric style was simple and severe. It was a stone version of the earlier thatched wooden temples. Doric columns were grooved or fluted and had a plain top, or capital. The column did not have a base. It stood flat on the floor stones.

The Ionic order was more delicate and decorative than the Doric style. The columns were taller and slimmer than the Doric. They were fluted, but they had a flattened rib between each flute. The capital was carved into a scroll shape. Ionic columns rested on a decorated base, or plinth. The plinth rested upon the floor stones.

The Corinthian style had fluted columns like the Ionic order. However, the capital was ornately carved into a pattern of curled acanthus leaves. Scrolls were sometimes added between the leaves.

Materials you will need:
Self-hardening clay or Plasticine, modeling tools or toothpicks, stiff cardboard, glue

Study the sketches of the three styles and decide which you want to model. You may want to model one column of each type. Or, you can make a single column or several columns topped by a beam.

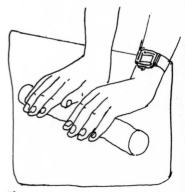

Figure 1

1. Roll thick columns out of self-hardening clay or Plasticine, as in Figure 1. Ours are ½ inch (1.75 cm) across and about 7 inches (18 cm) tall. Make them whatever size you prefer, but remember that they must stand upright. Do not make them too tall and thin.

2. Pat or roll out several thin, flat, tilelike pieces of clay for the floor stones, as in Figure 2. Your columns will rest on these.

Figure 2

3. For the capitals, model thick round discs, as in Figure 3. Also model several discs for the bases (plinths). Follow the drawings on page 8 to determine the shapes they should be.

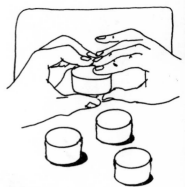

Figure 3

Figure 4

4. Use toothpicks or tools to do the fine modeling. Scoop out fluting on columns. Make acanthus leaves for the capital from tiny bits of clay pinched in with a tool, as in Figure 4. Fasten the clay leaves to the capital with a drop of water. Scrolls can be made by rolling a long "snake" out of clay and attaching one end to the front and one end to the back of the capital.

5. Join the capital and the rest of the column together by adding a drop of water between the pieces (Figure 5).

6. If you want a crossbeam over your columns, model a long rectangular member. Use a fine modeling tool or a toothpick to make decorative elements, as shown in Figure 6. After the beam is dry, glue it on top of three or four columns so that it extends just slightly beyond them.

7. Set all the shapes aside to harden thoroughly.

8. Glue the floor tiles to the cardboard base. Glue the columns to the tiles or base.

9. Assemble the building pieces. If the pieces do not stick together enough, use a drop of glue where needed. If you have used a dark-colored clay, paint your models white or light gray.

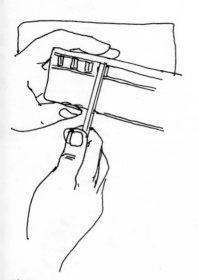

Figure 5

Figure 6

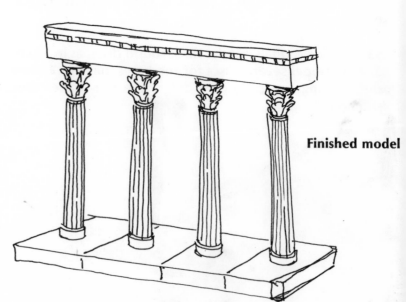

Finished model

Statues of Gods and Goddesses

By the fifth century B.C., most Greeks believed in a large number of gods and goddesses. They thought that the gods lived on Mount Olympus and that they obeyed their own laws and hierarchy. But the Greeks also believed that the gods had human feelings and participated in and interfered with human lives.

Some of the more important Greek gods and goddesses are described briefly below. Look them up in a reference book, before you decide which statue you want to make.

Materials you will need:
A wooden block for base, wire cutters and pliers, thick electrical wire, nail and hammer, spool or thread wire, strips of burlap or rags, plaster of Paris and bucket, spatula, rasp or file, sandpaper

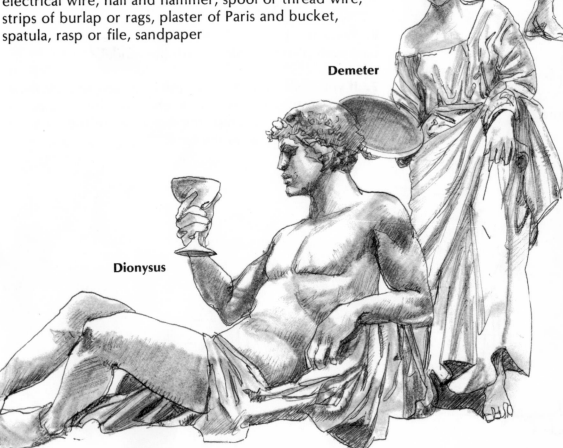

Aries

Demeter

Dionysus

11

Figure 1

Figure 2

1. Nail one end of the electrical wire to the center of the wooden block. Fashion the rest of the wire into a framework for your figure. Make it any size you like. To make arms, attach smaller pieces of wire to the shoulder areas with spool wire, as shown in Figure 1.

2. In the bucket, add water and then stir in plaster of Paris until it becomes thick enough to mound up like pudding on your spatula. You may have to let the plaster mixture sit for a few minutes so it thickens.

3. Cut or rip strips of fabric or burlap. Dip them in the plaster and wind them around the wire armature to build up the figure, as in Figure 2.

4. When the basic shape is formed, build up the details with pure plaster, using a spatula, as in Figure 3.

5. When the plaster hardens, use a rasp or file to smooth and define the features. Use sandpaper to smooth the surfaces.

6. Wipe the plaster off the wooden base, or cover the base with plaster to blend with the model.

7. If you wish, you can paint the hair, face, and clothing of your statue, the way it might have been done in ancient Greece. To finish the statue, write the name of the god or goddess on the base.

Figure 3

SOME OF THE GODS AND GODDESSES

Aphrodite: She was the goddess of beauty and of pure and ideal love. Often she is shown rising from the waters of the sea, where she was born.

Apollo: He was the son of Zeus and originally a sun god. He became a god of music, prophecy, and healing.

Ares: The god of war, he was a strong, powerful man usually shown wearing a helmet and breastplate and carrying a sword.

Artemis: She was the goddess of hunting and forests as well as the goddess of light and moonlight.

Athena: The daughter of Zeus, Athena was the goddess of war and of the arts of peace and knowledge.

Demeter: The goddess of the earth, she watched over agriculture and harvests.

Dionysus: The god of dancing, wine, and drunkenness, he is usually shown as a young man with a crown of grape leaves.

Hades: He was the god of the underworld. He is usually shown as a serious, older man.

Hephaestus: At first Hephaestus was the god of fire, thunder, and lightning. He later became the blacksmith god of Olympus.

Hera: Sister and wife of Zeus, she presided over marriage, maternity, and widowhood.

Hermes: He was the messenger of the gods and leader of souls to the underworld. Hermes was a great runner and the god of games of chance.

Hestia: She was the goddess of womanhood and the guardian of the city-state. Fire or a lamp are symbols identified with her.

Pan: He was the god of nature, forests, and mountains. He is usually depicted with the body and head of a man and the legs and ears of a goat.

Poseidon: Poseidon was the god of the seas and waters and of earthquakes. He is almost always shown holding a trident.

Zeus: Zeus was the supreme ruler and god of the sky and weather. He is usually shown holding a scepter in his left hand and a thunderbolt in his right.

Poseidon   Athena   Pan   Hera   Apollo

An Ancient Stringed Instrument

The Greek lyre was similar to the harp. It had seven strings stretched on a frame, with a base made of tortoise shell. The Greeks believed that Apollo, the god of music, entertained the other gods on Mount Olympus with his playing. He is usually shown in art works playing or holding the lyre.

Learning to play the lyre was an essential part of a Greek boy's education. In contests, games, and the theater, men and boys sang poems to the accompaniment of the lyre. Only the words of Greek poetry remain. We have no record of how their music sounded.

Materials you will need:
A heavy wire coat hanger, lightweight cardboard, felt-tip pen or crayons, tape, scissors, seven narrow rubber bands or heavyweight nylon fishing line

1. Cut a piece of cardboard into a rectangle that is 6 inches by 8 inches (15 cm × 20 cm).

2. Within this rectangle, draw the tortoise shell shape shown in Figure 1. Cut around the shape. Then color it in with the tortoise shell pattern shown in Figure 2.

3. Bend a coat hanger into a round, smooth shape as shown in Figure 3.

4. Turn it, hook down, and bend it into the shape shown in Figure 4. Make the distance between the points about 6 inches (15 cm).

5. Cut the rubber bands open, or cut lengths of fishing line. Tie seven pieces tightly between the bridge and the hanger hook, as in Figure 5. Cut off the excess strings.

6. Tape the back of the tortoise shell to the hook so it looks like Figure 6.

7. Play by plucking the strings. You can change the pitch of the strings. To make the pitch higher, bend the hook outward, toward you, to tighten the strings. To lower the pitch, loosen the strings. Or re-tie the strings to change their tightness and pitch. Or, you can pinch a string in the middle before plucking it to raise the pitch.

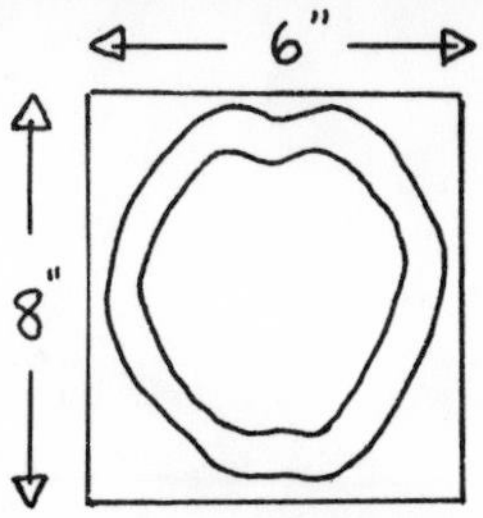

← 6" →

8"

Figure 1

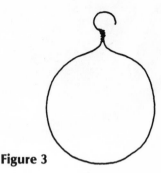

Figure 2

Figure 3

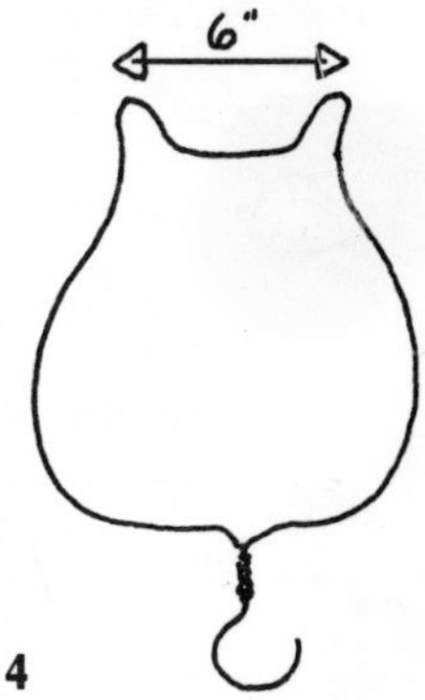

← 6" →

Figure 4

BRIDGE

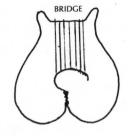

Figure 5

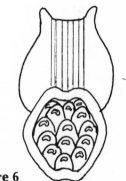

Figure 6

15

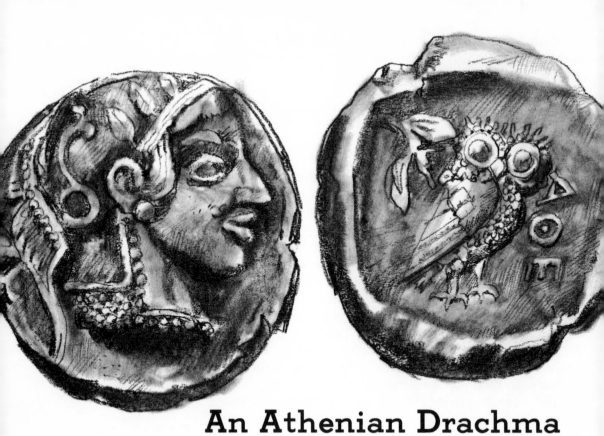

An Athenian Drachma

The early Greeks traded with bronze tripods, axes, rings, and bundles of iron nails instead of money. By the end of the seventh century B.C., their main currency was a coin called the *drachma*, meaning handful. Each city minted its own drachmae. Silver coins from Athens showed the head of the goddess Athena, the patron of the city, on one side. The other side showed her sacred owl. Along with the owl there was often an olive branch, a symbol of peace and prosperity.

Coins were also made of gold or electrum, a mixture of silver and gold. The smallest Greek coin was called an *obol*. Six obols were equal to one drachma.

Materials you will need:
Self-hardening clay, small modeling tools and toothpicks, silver or gold paint, black paint or a black felt-tip pen, a flat wire rack for drying the coins

1. Model several flat discs about 1 inch (2.5 cm) in diameter and about as thick as your finger, as in Figure 1.

2. Use the toothpick to sketch a woman's helmeted head on one side. (See Figure 2.) Sketch an owl on the other side. Use a tool to scrape away some of the background from the shapes you have drawn, leaving them slightly in relief. If you prefer, the designs can simply be scratched into the surfaces.

3. Place the pieces on a wire rack to dry.

4. When they are thoroughly dry, paint the coins. (See Figure 3.) If the grooves in the scratched designs fill in with paint, go over them with black paint and a fine brush. Or use a permanent black felt-tip pen with a fine point. Leave the edges of the coins rough, as the originals were. Do not sand or smooth them.

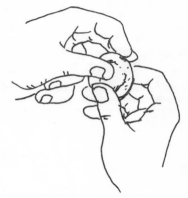

Figure 1

Figure 2

Figure 3

A Scarf
with Printed Borders

In ancient Greece, girls wore a shawl-scarf, similar to what we call a cloak, decorated with border motifs as a head covering. Men wore a *chlamys*, or cape, also decorated with border designs. Women and girls spun, dyed, and wove the wool or linen cloth for the cloaks, garments, and blankets they used in their everyday lives. Colored dyes were made from plants and even from whelks, small sea snails that make a rich purple-red color. The fabrics were often embroidered with favorite motifs repeated in the woven work. The designs shown are adapted from Greek designs. These designs will be used to make our scarf, though the border is printed rather than woven.

Materials you will need:
A large art gum or soap eraser 2 inches × 3 inches (5 cm × 7.5 cm) or a medium-sized potato cut in half, block printing tools (v-gouge), Exacto or mat knife, paintbrush, paper, pencil, fabric paint (of tempera consistency), soft cotton fabric 12 inches × 36 inches (30 cm × 90 cm)

1. Cut the fabric and hem the edges. Iron the fabric flat.

2. On paper, draw around the outer edge of the eraser or potato half (blotted dry).

3. On the paper, copy one of the Greek designs within the drawn shape. You may prefer to trace the design.

4. Transfer the design onto the eraser or potato, using a paintbrush. (See Figure 1.) (Do not use a pencil, because it will scratch the surface.)

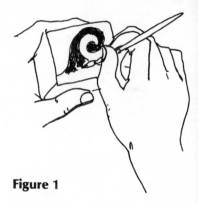

Figure 1

5. Cut straight down about ¼ inch (.5 cm) around the outlines of the shapes with the knife.

6. Use the v-gouge to cut away all the background areas, leaving only the raised design, as in Figure 2.

7. Brush paint over the raised surface.

8. Place the eraser or potato printing block paint side down on the border of the fabric. Press evenly and firmly to make the impression. (See Figure 3.)

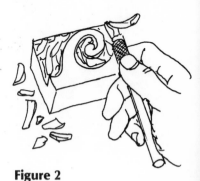

Figure 2

9. Repeat, but be sure to line the second print up exactly alongside the first, so that the border connects as in the sketches shown in Figure 4. Make the border design all around the edges of the front side of the scarf.

10. Follow the directions on the box of fabric paint. They will tell you how to set the color permanently. (Some paints require ironing to set them.)

11. To make "red-figure" or "black-figure" designs, use black or terra-cotta colored cloth and the opposite color paint.

Figure 3

Figure 4

Tasty Greek Salad

In ancient Greece, breakfast and lunch often consisted of fruit, cheese, wine, and bread. The bread was usually made of coarsely ground barley grain. The first course of the main evening meal was generally fish and vegetables, such as peas, beans, leeks, or cabbage. This course was followed by fruits such as figs, grapes, citrus fruits or dates, and honey-flavored cakes. Meat—especially lamb—was served primarily at festivals. Food was served on plates made of metal or pottery. Spoons and knives were the only eating utensils.

The ingredients in our salad recipe were as common and popular with the ancient Greeks as they are today in modern Greece.

Materials you will need:
Lettuce—freshly washed leaves, dried
Feta cheese—drained and crumbled
Black and green olives—pitted and sliced
Basil leaves—washed and torn into pieces
Fresh oregano or marjoram leaves, or a pinch of each, dried
Olive oil
Juice from a fresh lemon

1. In a large bowl, combine several handfuls of lettuce with two or three tablespoons of feta cheese, a handful of olives, and some basil and oregano or marjoram.

2. Sprinkle the top lightly with a couple of tablespoons of olive oil and lemon juice.

3. Toss the ingredients together to mix them.

4. Serve with crusty bread.

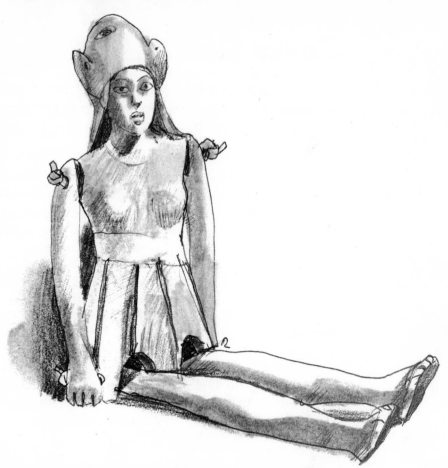

A Doll with Movable Arms and Legs

The ancient Greeks made toys for their children, including model boats, wagons, dolls, doll houses, toy soldiers, small animals, balls (wool stuffed inside animal skin), tops, and hoops. Many of these have survived and may be seen in museums. Among them is a clay doll with movable joints held together with string. The doll is probably a model of a goddess (perhaps Athena) wearing a three-part crown. It most likely dates from the fourth century B.C.

Materials you will need:
Self-hardening clay or papier-mâché (see box),
thin knitting needle or long embroidery needle, string,
ruler, scissors, wax, paints (optional)

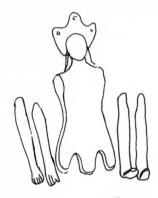

Figure 1

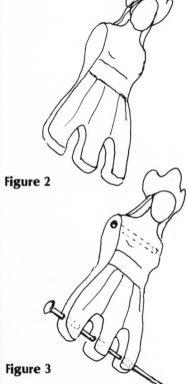

Figure 2

Figure 3

Figure 4

1. Use papier-mâché or clay to model the doll in five pieces. The pieces should be two arms, two legs, and a combined head and trunk, as in Figure 1. You can make the doll any size you wish. Ours has a body measuring 4 inches (10 cm) from the top of the crown to the bottom of the skirt.

2. Make the shoulder area about 1 inch (2.5 cm) wide and about ¾ inch (2 cm) thick. Model the curves in the skirt as in Figure 2. These will hold the tops of the legs. Shape the top end of the body into a neck and head. Use modeling tools or a toothpick to add features to the face.

3. Make the arms 2½ inches (6 cm) long and the legs 3 inches (7.5 cm) long. The legs and arms are narrow at the top. The rest of their length should be about ½ inch (1 cm) thick.

4. Use the needle to make holes through the tops of the arms and legs. Be sure to leave enough material around each hole so it is strong. Poke the needle through the three skirt panels and through the shoulders, as in Figure 3. Let the pieces dry thoroughly.

5. The dry pieces can be sanded to smooth any rough edges. You can paint the pieces with tempera or acrylics, or you may leave them plain.

6. To attach the pieces, dip one end of the string in melted wax to stiffen it, or thread it through an embroidery needle. Push the string through the holes and parts as shown in Figure 4. Tie fat double knots in the string to keep the ends from slipping through the holes.

PAPIER-MÂCHÉ MIX
Use either white glue or wallpaper paste mixture. If using white glue, mix ⅔ glue with ⅓ water to make a creamy mixture. Wallpaper paste is usually mixed 1 part powder to 10 parts water (but follow direction on the box). Sometimes you may need to add more powder to get a slightly thicker mixture.

Making a Greek Tunic

Both men and women wore a basic garment, the *chiton*. This was a loose-fitting, flowing tunic which can be made from two rectangular pieces of linen or muslin sewn together. Holes were left for the head and the arms. The tunic was tied at the waist. Chitons were often dyed. Red and yellow were the most popular colors. Women's chitons were longer and fuller than men's. Both men and women wore sandals.

Materials you will need:
Soft, easily draped fabric or an old sheet, needle and thread, straight pins, tape measure, belt or rope, chalk, safety pins

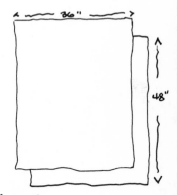

Figure 1

1. To determine the length, have someone measure the distance from the base of your neck to where you want the tunic to end.

2. Cut two panels. In this example, the width is 36 inches (90 cm) and the length is 48 inches (120 cm) (see Figure 1). Sew the panels all the way up the long sides, wrong side out, making a 1-inch (2.5-cm) seam. Or fold a sheet in half and cut it to the right dimensions. (See Figure 2.) Sew up one edge (the edge opposite the fold), and turn it right side out.

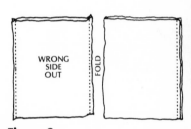

Figure 2

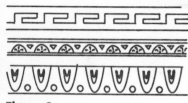

Figure 3

3. On the right side, decorate the edges with a border design. (See Figure 3.) Or, if you wish, dye the cloth a color that you like.

4. Measure and mark with chalk the middle of the top edge of the front and back panels 18 inches (45 cm) in from the side. (See Figure 4.) Mark points A and B 4 inches (10 cm) out to each side. The neck opening is between these points, and the armholes are to each side (between points A and C and B and D).

5. Slip the chiton over your head, bringing the top edge just below the armpits. At points A and B, pull the front and back edges up onto the shoulders and fasten them together with a safety pin. (See Figure 5.) Pin the arms together just under the armpit.

6. Tie a belt or rope around your waist. Blouse the fabric up over the belt until the chiton is loose and comfortable.

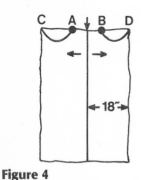

Figure 4

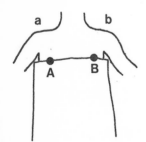

Figure 5

Knucklebones:
A Game of Skill

Knucklebones was a popular game of skill in ancient Greece for both children and adults. Sometimes knucklebones were given as a reward to well-behaved children. The game of knucklebones was similar to our game of jacks, except that it was played without a ball. The Greeks used bleached knucklebones or neck vertebrae, probably from a lamb or sheep. These were roughly 1 inch (2.5 cm) cubes with bony protrusions. Sometimes five bones were used. At other times, nine were used.

The object of the game is to toss one bone into the air, pick up the others, and then catch the first bone before it falls, *all with one hand.*

Knucklebones was also a dice game played with only four bones. The pieces always had four flat sides plus two ends. When used as dice, the best throw—when each die landed differently—was called "Aphrodite," after the goddess of love and beauty. The worst throw—when they all landed alike—was called "the dog." Scenes showing people playing knucklebones are frequently found on pottery and on wall paintings.

Materials you will need:
The neck of a chicken, turkey, or other fowl, pebbles, an empty can, laundry bleach

Figure 1

TO MAKE YOUR KNUCKLEBONES

1. Boil the fowl neck until the meat can be picked off easily.

2. Pull off the meat. Then separate the bones from each other at the natural joints.

3. Clean the bones.

4. Place the bones in a can to soak, covered with bleach, for several hours or overnight. (See Figure 1.)

5. Wash and dry the bones. Use as many as you like—up to ten.

6. Chicken neck bones tend to be too light. To weight them, glue a tiny stone inside each bone before playing.

TO PLAY THE GAME

1. To determine which player goes first, each player in turn tosses all the bones at once to see how many he or she can catch on the back of his or her hand before they fall. The player who catches the most goes first.

2. To play, toss all the bones onto a smooth, hard surface such as the floor or a table.

3. Throw one bone up into the air. With one hand, pick up one of the bones lying on the floor. Then catch the airborne bone before it falls. (See Figure 2.)

4. Continue to toss and pick up bones one by one. Put them aside until all have been gathered.

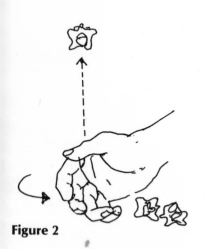

Figure 2

5. Proceed to toss and pick up bones by twos, then threes, and so on, until at last you toss and gather all the bones at once. If the tossed bone falls before you complete your move, you lose and the next player goes. Whoever picks up all the bones first wins.

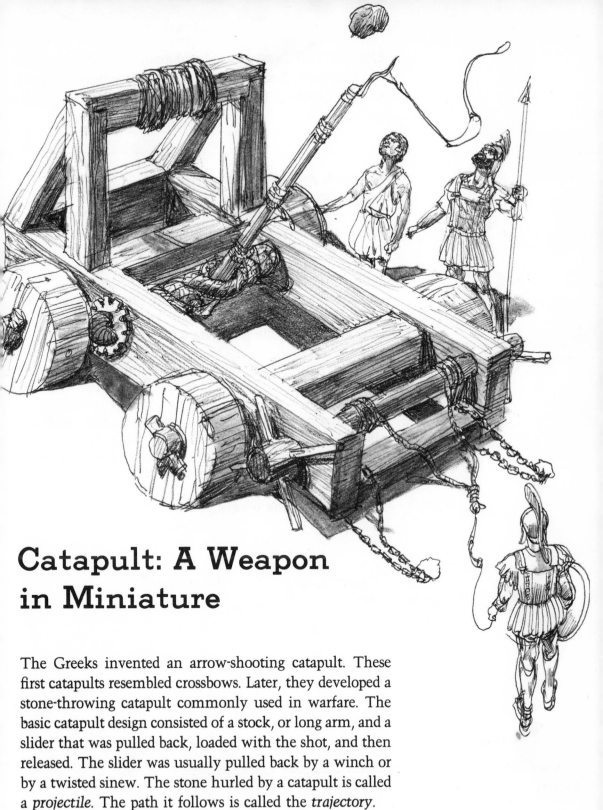

Catapult: A Weapon in Miniature

The Greeks invented an arrow-shooting catapult. These first catapults resembled crossbows. Later, they developed a stone-throwing catapult commonly used in warfare. The basic catapult design consisted of a stock, or long arm, and a slider that was pulled back, loaded with the shot, and then released. The slider was usually pulled back by a winch or by a twisted sinew. The stone hurled by a catapult is called a *projectile*. The path it follows is called the *trajectory*.

When Alexander the Great besieged Tyre in 332 B.C., he shook the walls of the town with huge stones tossed from a catapult. Still later, the Macedonian general Demetrius built catapults that could hurl stones that weighed as much as 175 pounds (80 kg) and had a range of about 55 feet (16.72 m).

Materials you will need:
A wire coat hanger, wire cutters, pliers, tape measure, ruler, permanent marking pen (a laundry marker, for example), plastic spoon, cork, strong rubber band 2 ¾ inches × ¼ inch (7 cm × .5 cm)

1. Use wire cutters to cut the hook off the hanger at the two points shown in Figure 1. If the wire is hard to cut, twist the wire while pinching with the cutters.

2. Use pliers to straighten the whole length of the wire.

3. Bring the ends of the wire evenly together, making a curve, as shown in Figure 2. Do not pinch the curve too tightly because it will later be straightened again. Use the marking pen to show the center of the curve.

4. Straighten the wire.

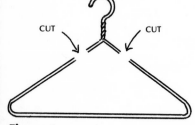

CUT   CUT

Figure 1

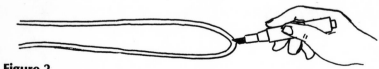

Figure 2

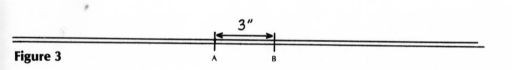

3"

Figure 3

A   B

5. Measure and mark points A and B 1 ½ inches (3 cm) out from each side of the middle mark, as shown in Figure 3.

6. Use the pliers, as shown in Figure 4, to bend a right angle in the wire at points A and B (see Figure 5). Check to see that the wire legs are straight.

7. Measure and mark points C and D each 1 inch (2 cm) back from corners A and B. Mark points E and F each 3 inches (7.5 cm) back from points C and D, as shown in Figure 5.

8. Use the pliers to bend the wires over at points C and D. Bend them again *in the same direction* at points E and F, as shown in Figure 6. Set the bent wire directly over the diagram pattern (see Figure 7) and bend until wire angles are the same as those in this book. Straighten the legs to be sure that they lie flat on the table.

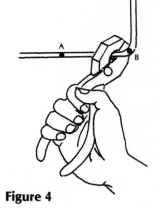

Figure 4

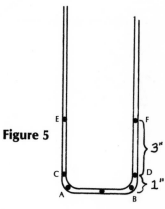

Figure 5

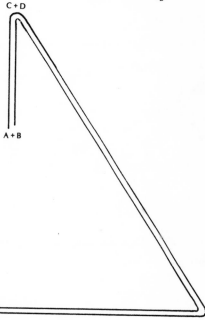

Figure 6

Figure 7

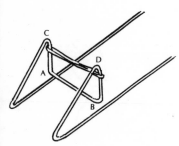

Figure 8

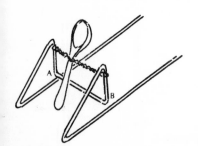

Figure 9

9. Slip the rubber band over points A and B, resting it across the top of C and D (see Figure 8). Our model uses a twisted rubber band instead of the hide or sinews the Greeks used for powering the catapult.

10. Twist the rubber band until it is tightly wound.

11. Insert the spoon, handle down, with the concave side of the bowl facing out, between the rubber band legs. Position the spoon handle so that it hits bar A-B. (See Figure 9.)

12. For a projectile, use a cork or a wad of paper or papier-mâché painted to look like a boulder. Do not use anything hard that could hit and injure another person. Bend the spoon bowl back until it rests upside down on the table. Put the projectile in the bowl of the spoon and let it go. You can experiment with different trajectories by changing the position of the spoon handle. Or you can vary the number of twists of the band and the angles of the bent wire (see Figure 10). *DO NOT AIM AT PEOPLE!*

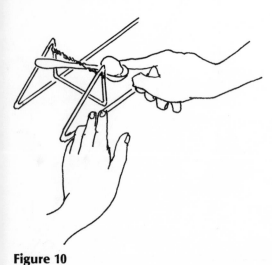

Figure 10

A	alpha	H	eta	N	nu	T	tau
B	beta	Θ	theta	Ξ	xi	Y	upsilon
Γ	gamma	I	iota	O	omicron	Φ	phi
Δ	delta	K	kappa	Π	pi	X	chi
E	epsilon	Λ	lambda	P	rho	Ψ	psi
Z	zeta	M	mu	Σ	sigma	Ω	omega

Alphabet Scroll

The Greek alphabet developed out of the writing of the ancient Phoenicians, who first used individual letters or symbols to stand for separate sounds. The word alphabet originates from *alpha* and *beta*, the first two letters of the Greek alphabet. Modern Greek is still written with the ancient letters, and the letters are also used as symbols all over the world in many branches of science and mathematics.

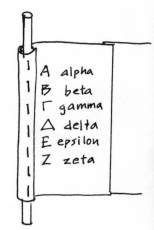

Figure 1

Materials you will need:
Several sheets of paper (typing paper or slightly larger), invisible tape or glue, two dowels or wooden sticks that are slightly longer than the paper, stapler, ribbon, pen

1. Use tape or glue to fasten several sheets of paper together side by side into one long sheet.

2. Staple each short end of the long paper strip to the middle of a wooden pole as shown in Figure 1. Then roll the scroll inwards toward the center. Roll half the paper on each pole.

3. Tie the scroll together with a ribbon as in Figure 2.

4. Unroll the scroll and hold the paper flat by placing a weight at each end if it starts to roll up. Copy the Greek alphabet symbols and their English names on the paper.

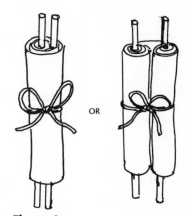

Figure 2

Index